Manipulation Tactics

10 Techniques to Influence Human Psychology & Behavior, Understand How People Manipulate, and Effectively Use Persuasion to Your Advantage!

Nick Anderson

Table of Contents:

Introduction 3
Chapter 1: Offering an Alternative View or Reading of Reality 32
Chapter 2: Denial 45
Chapter 3: Tapping the Power of Shame 52
Chapter 4: Diversion 60
Chapter 5: Seduction 66
Chapter 6: Minimization 77
Chapter 7: Guilt Trips 84
Chapter 8: Rationalization 92
Chapter 9: Gaslighting 100
Chapter 10: Play the Victim 112
Conclusion 118

Introduction

What is manipulation? Manipulation is using all sorts of tactics to control the behavior and emotions of other people. It also involves using all sorts of tactics to control your relationships.

You have to understand that whenever two people get together, there is a power struggle. You are reading signals into each other and you are ultimately trying to contain and direct each other.

Now, this can be friendly, this can be positive like in a family, but even then, in that context, there is some sort of manipulation because hey, let's face it, if you were dealing with other people who have their own agenda, in many cases, it's a recipe for chaos. This is especially true if you're dealing with children.

Parents learn early on how to manipulate their kids. It also works the other way. Kids from an early age learn to read their parents and they know how to emotionally manipulate their parents as well.

So, there is this power struggle regarding manipulation. It starts in the home, and it spills over into all our other relationships whether it's in school or at work.

And here's the thing about manipulation. It is not inherently bad or good. It all depends on what your motivations are.

And the worst thing you can do is to assume that manipulation is just always bad. That you should run away from it and that you should not practice it. Well, here's the problem. If you fail to learn how manipulation works and you're completely blind to it, you are more likely to be manipulated by other people.

At the end of the day, manipulation is part of the human experience. The issue is how to use it in such a way that it leads to common goals and produces a net positive social good.

Why Do People Manipulate?

Well, there are many different motivations for manipulation and, at the end of the day, it really is all about trying to get another person to think or do what you want them to think or do.

In other words, it deals with the core human reality that all of us have our own agenda. All of us have our own path. All of us have our own capabilities for learning, loving, and getting along with others. And in many cases, there will always be conflicts because you may not necessarily be aware of or even agree with somebody else's agenda.

So what do you do in that situation? This is where manipulation comes in.

Now, the word "manipulation" has a very negative connotation. In an American context, it's usually viewed as some sort of imposition of one person's will over another. It's as if you are trying to get that person to do something that they normally would not want to do.

Well, this is not always the case. In fact, in many cases, people are just unaware of the options available to them. And in many situations, they think that the options available, as far as certain situations are concerned, are limited to options that are actually quite harmful or are not all that optimal.

What do you in that situation? By using manipulation techniques, you might actually open their minds to another possibility that leads to better productivity, better results, and a better life.

Now, you may be thinking to yourself, "That sounds great and everything, but manipulation doesn't apply to me. I don't want to be manipulated, and I don't want to manipulate other people." Fair enough.

But you have to understand that when you are exposed to the world in all its different forms of media, you are being manipulated. In fact, politics is the art of manipulation. Advertisements are the product of billions of dollars in annual budgets intended to get people to change their behavior no matter how slightly.

Manipulation is all around you and it doesn't really help anybody to pretend that it doesn't exist or to imagine themselves as somehow exempt from it. The truth is, being aware of how people get others to think of certain things or to follow certain directives is a good first step to learning how to be a more effective human being.

Because at the end of the day, since we are dealing with a complex society where everybody else has conflicting goals and aims and desires, it's a good idea to see if you're being manipulated and if you're going to go along with it.

In many cases, when you are being manipulated, you might actually find yourself in a process where your eyes are being opened to possibilities that you didn't think existed. That may be a good thing.

Maybe you developed tunnel vision early on. Maybe your parents had a certain value set that kind of robbed you of the full set of possibilities that the world has to offer. And when you come across people that have a different mindset and they have these persuasion skills, you become better because you were exposed to these individuals and they, at some level or another, manipulated you. It doesn't necessarily have to be a bad thing.

So, before we jump into the inner workings of the art of manipulating others and how to produce a net positive good with it, let's get down to the basics. Let's start with motivations.

Why Do People Try to Manipulate?

Well, it all boils down to a spectrum of motives. You have to understand that motivations really assume their color depending on your perspective.

Something could be very negative when viewed from a particular angle and at a particular time. But when you look at it from a different situation, it might actually be quite positive. So, generally speaking, when people manipulate, it really is all about hierarchy.

And I hate to say it, but the basic human hierarchy involves somebody at the top and somebody at the bottom. In other words, superiority and inferiority.

Some people manipulate because they feel that they're superior. They feel that they have something over other people because they're able to convince them to think and feel a certain way, as well as perform certain actions. This then has a feedback effect of feeling in control.

Now, this might seem negative, but in certain contexts, it's actually quite positive. You have to understand that a lot people who feel that they have lost power over their lives feel a tremendous sense of satisfaction when they're able to gain a sense of control when they're able to influence others.

Others do it for power. And again, that concept of "power" is quite vague because different people looking at it from different perspectives might define power in context.

Some people look at power as a way of extracting money, sexual favors, physical actions, social connections, and control from other people. Others view power as a sense of being able to give and serve and improve the other people around them.

Again, it's all a question of perspective, but they all have a common trait involving manipulation. Because to get the energy and willpower you need to learn the ins and outs of manipulation, you have to be motivated for a fairly extended period of time.

Being able to get others to do what you want them to do or to look at the situation from your perspective doesn't happen overnight. It's definitely not the product of some sort of cosmic lottery. It doesn't fall into your lap. It's something that you work on over a longer period of time.

Let me tell you, whenever you're building any kind of skill, there are all sorts of ups and downs. It's not a straight shot at all. And manipulation, persuasion, and the ability to just be a more convincing human being requires this kind of dedication. That's why you have to have that motivation.

And it's very easy to look at this as all negative and as an egotistic or even narcissistic project, but those are judgments. Just as a murderer would use a knife to kill somebody, a surgeon can use the same knife to save somebody's life. Manipulation, at the end of the day, is a tool.

So, it all depends on your ultimate motivation and the price you're willing to pay to be able to wield that tool the right way. And it takes a lot of time. It takes a lot of practice. There are many misunderstandings that you have to weather and overcome.

But the good news is, once you master the art of manipulation, persuasion and influence, you can be a force for good.

Be Clear About Your Psychological State

Now, let's face it, a lot of us come from different backgrounds. Some people have abusive backgrounds. Maybe they're survivors of emotional abuse, maybe they survived all sorts of physically abusive conditions. A lot of people had to survive sexual abuse, and a lot of these past experiences create traumatic reactions that color our motivations.

You have to be clear on why you're doing something, and that can only make sense based on what you think you know about yourself.

You might think that you are an unattractive person. You might think you're fat and nobody would love you or would want to be friends with you with the right motives. You might think that you're just a tool to be used by other people. But a lot of this thinking is actually inherited from your parents, the people who took care of you, and the people who were around you during your formative years.

The question is, are these valid readings of what actually happened? And even if they were, why do you choose to hang on to them if they harm you? Why do you choose to entertain them if they hold you back and rob you of your ability to live up to your fullest potential as a human being?

These are key questions that we need to ask as adults. It's hard to ask these questions when we are children. But eventually, you know you have become an adult when you start asking yourself these fundamental questions.

You are not your past. You are not what other people think of you. You are not what you think your limitations are. You're more valuable than that, and it's ultimately your choice of who you want to be.

I want to get this out of the way because when people have all sorts of distorted ideas of who they are, what they're capable of, and what their off-limit areas are as far as their life goes, these are all manifested in personality disorders.

There are a lot of people who are very controlling. There are individuals that are addicted to drama that cannot survive without creating chaos. It's not because they're inherently evil, but this is how they make sense of the world.

There are others who are passive aggressive. They could tell you one thing to your face, and another when your back is turned. Now this doesn't necessarily mean that they're bad people, but their world is colored a certain way and is based on what they know.

If you want to become a more persuasive person, the first step is to come up with a mental diagnostic of how you view the world and how you see yourself in that world. Can you explain yourself? Can you explain why you think the way you think? Can you explain why you value yourself a certain way and how you define your personality?

I know this is kind of a tall order because this requires asking fundamental questions that people may not be all that comfortable with. Because for the longest time, you might think that you were an okay person, but it turns out that, from an objective perspective, you cause a lot of hurt. You harm people. You cause a lot of pain.

And it takes a lot of self-delusion to think that that's okay. And to interpret the loss, the pain, the misunderstanding, the harm, into something that doesn't strike close to home, it actually takes quite a bit of psychological as well as emotional energy to do that.

But instead of playing these games with yourself, why not harness that power to produce better results for others? This is why you have to look into the kind of personality that you already have and let the chips fall where they may.

You may discover certain things that may be uncomfortable. These things might get under your skin. They might corrode who you think you are and what you're capable of.

A lot of people who use manipulation for destructive ends tend to suffer from antisocial personality. Now, forget the label. Usually, when we think about antisocial, we think about somebody who is very reclusive or even introverted. That's not what antisocial personality is as far as classical psychology goes.

Antisocial personality involves a set of personality traits that drive people to cause harm to others. They know that the things that they say harms other people and diminishes them, discourages them, or even destroys their self-esteem, but they can't help it. They set these things in motion like some sort of snowball effect.

The same applies to borderline personality. You have this tendency for chaos. You can't quite put your finger on it, but you just feel that you are not complete unless somebody's suffering or somebody's doubting themselves or somebody's feeling conflicted because deep down inside, you feel conflicted.

The idea is "Why should I be miserable alone when I can cause misery for other people?" It's sick, it's twisted, and it sounds harsh. But unless you're honest with yourself that this is how your personality is configured, you're not going to look at persuasive skills with a clear set of eyes.

I'm not trying to ask you to get psychological help or get professional help so you can be healed. Instead, I'm asking for something more practical. I'm saying that you should look at this situation from a specific lens.

The time is now to take the opportunity to look at the lens. Do you have low self-esteem? Do you have a low sense of self-worth? Are you a survivor of past trauma that led to antisocial behavior or personality? Do you have a borderline personality?

Now, go beyond the labels and look at the lens. Own that lens. Understand that this is who you are right now.

I'm not saying that you can't choose to be another person later on. Maybe you want to let go of that antisocial personality disorder, and that would be awesome. But what's important as far as our present objective is concerned is to take ownership of who you are right now.

Do you like causing problems? Do you like drama? Are you addicted to feeling good when bad things happen to other people? That's okay. Accept that. That's part of who you are.

Because unless you look at yourself with clear eyes and take ownership of the lens you use to make sense of the rest of the world, the techniques that I'm going to teach you in this book is not going to work. There will always be a sense of detachment there.

So, you have to take full ownership of your motivations. And once you're able to do that, you can then set them aside and pay close attention to the techniques so that you can possibly choose a better outcome.

How to Tell If You're Being Manipulated

As I have mentioned in the introduction to this book, manipulation is a constant. When you open your browser or your mobile device and you come across an ad, you're being manipulated. When you watch a video, you're being manipulated.

The sounds that you hear when you watch a scene on YouTube is intentional. They could have easily used different music. Why did they choose that particular track? Why are they looking at the story from a particular perspective? None of this happens by random.

The problem is, a lot of people are clueless regarding manipulation techniques because they assume that what they're seeing is somehow natural. At the back of their heads, they're thinking that this is the way it should be. Well, manipulation is all about placing triggers in a strategic way so that it affects how people interpret those triggers.

Please understand that the world's stimuli are inherently neutral. I know that's a controversial statement because when you look at a burning building, for example, and you see a pillar of smoke, orange flames coming out, people screaming from the windows, and possibly even people falling down, it's very easy to get triggered.

It's very easy to get the sense that there is something horrible going on and this is the end of the world for those people. You're being emotional when you do that.

But when you respond that way, what do you think will happen? If it is the end of the world and it is the worst-case scenario, what do you think will happen as far as your personal capability goes in dealing with that situation?

Chances are, you probably would freak out. Chances are, if you're right there on the scene and you can sense the heat, you can smell the smoke, and you can feel the hopelessness, despair and chaos, you would run around like a chicken with its head cut off.

In other words, you would be worthless and useless. But you would fit in perfectly because everybody else is doing the same thing. They're being useless. They're not dealing with the situation in a productive way.

Now, what if you looked at the same set of stimuli and you interpret it as a challenge that can be handled? Well, if that's your mindset, you would be able to resist the almost overwhelming temptation to run around like a chicken with its head cut off.

Instead, there's a higher likelihood that you would casually whip out your mobile phone and call the local fire department. And after a few minutes, the firetrucks come, the fire is put out, and everybody is taken to the hospital or everybody is taken care of.

Now, which mindset led to a better result? It should be obvious.

But here's the thing. Both sets of stimuli are the same. The only difference is how we interpreted the stimuli. There's still a pillar of smoke, there's still orange flames, there are still people screaming, but our interpretation of these external factors that we can see, hear, touch, taste and smell vary from person to person.

My point is, the way you mentally process this information shapes your reality. In fact, it dictates your reality. This is the difference between rich people and poor people. This is the difference between people who are in loving, supportive and nurturing relationships and those in dysfunctional relationships.

It all boils down to mindset. And mindset is crucial when it comes to manipulation.

Because if you want to get people to do something that they normally wouldn't do, you have to take control of this mechanism. You have to zero in on their interpretation or their read of the external stimuli so they feel a certain range of emotions.

This range of emotions doesn't happen in a vacuum. It has an impact on the things you choose to do.

Let me tell you, the world doesn't give a damn what your intentions are. I know that sounds harsh because hey, a lot of us would love to be judged by our intentions. In fact, I would argue that most people would love to be evaluated based on what they wanted to do, what they could have done, should have done, or could have done.

What a wonderful world that would be because in that wonderful fantasy world, everybody would be compensated based on their potential and based on the things that they hoped and wished they could have done.

But we live in the real world. In the real world, you get judged by your results. Your boss couldn't care less what your intentions are. All your boss cares about is what she could see; that you do your work; that you hit the goal; that you sell the property; that you produce the book; that you deliver the goods; and so on and so forth. Results.

But if you pay attention to what I just said and the process that reality takes, from the idea, to the perception, to the emotional state, to the action, you have a lot more control over your results than you give yourself credit for.

Failures, losers, bums, the people that society would like to marginalize, are just people who either forgot this process or willfully ignore it. These are people who spend their time saying, "What happened? What happened to my life? What happened to me? What happened to our relationship? What happened to my job? Why am I making this much money when I could be making so much more? The rich are getting richer and the poor are getting poorer."

These are the people who ask what happened. And that's because of their mindset. A little change in that mindset and a little alteration in the personal narrative can turn them into people who make things happen.

And it really all boils down to how you choose to perceive reality because it's all a choice. It's not inherited from your parents. It's not locked into your genes. It's something that you willfully took up.

Now, what makes this tricky is the fact that while it started out as a choice, through prolonged exposure, it eventually becomes habitual. In fact, you grow so accustomed to this way of thinking about and processing reality that you feel that this is reality. But at its root, it's a choice.

It's not much different from seeing that building on fire. It doesn't have to be the end of the world. It doesn't have to be the worst-case scenario. That's a choice. That's an interpretation.

Another classic example of this is two people seeing a Ferrari. Two guys are at a street corner and they see a Ferrari stop at the stop light.

One guy looks at that awesome piece of Italian automotive engineering and says to himself, "There's no way I can buy a car like that. Not in a million lifetimes. The rich are getting richer. The poor are getting poorer. Life is unfair. That sucks."

The other guy looks at the same car and instead of making some judgment about his personal capabilities, says to himself, "How can I afford a car like that?"

Now, let me ask you, what is more empowering? Which leads to more doors of opportunity? Which leads to more solutions? Which can be a gateway to greater and greater levels of motivation that can possibly lead to a breakthrough or even victory?

Well, let me tell you, it's not the first mindset. Because when you look at the statements the first person was making to himself, he's basically condemning himself. They're basically looking at what's going on as a judgment of their own personal capability.

They're no longer looking at themselves as potential owners of that Ferrari. Instead, they rebranded and defined themselves as somebody who's incapable of achieving that kind of reality.

The other person asked a question. When you ask a question, it's only a matter of time until you get an answer.

And questions can have different answers. In other words, there's a possibility. You haven't closed the door. You can trigger a chain reaction of actions that can eventually lead you to achieving one reality instead of another.

This is the difference. And it's crucial because at the end of the day, as I mentioned, the world is full of neutral stimuli and it's our interpretation that turn them into reality.

You chose your reality. And to manipulate other people, you have to learn how to work with that mindset so they choose your interpretation. This feedback is all about setting up the necessary conditions for the signals to be interpreted a certain way.

It's very easy to look at this whole process and entirely negative. I'm sure that if you've ever been in a manipulative relationship, either with your parents or with a romantic partner, you didn't appreciate the use of blame, guilt, or justifications to get you to a certain emotional state. Few people would. But that's just one way of manipulation.

You see, there's a thin line separating manipulation and persuasion. And as much as possible, I would like to use the term persuasion because it seems more positive.

But at the end of the day, manipulation and persuasion are really the same thing. It's all about using certain stimuli to color a person's read of the stimuli so that when they process it with their own internal belief systems, they feel a certain way and they act on that range of emotions to produce an outcome.

You know you're a persuasive person when the outcome that they arrive at is what you had in mind. Now, there are many ways to do this. You can appeal to a person's highest values.

A lot of Marxist scholars have been dumbfounded by the American experience. It's completely different from Europe. In Europe, it's easy to see how classes struggle, and a person's appreciation of their class station in life translates to politics.

In England, for example, working class people historically have voted for the labor party and big government initiatives because they feel that the labor party's policies of greater regulation, greater economic control, and wealth redistribution lines up with their class interests.

This is classic Marxist analysis. And in some European contexts, it works. Everything lines up. Not in the United States.

Scholars, as early as Thorstein Veblen, noticed something peculiar about the American experience with concepts like class. It turned out that in the United States, the poorer a person is, the more market-oriented or forward-driven their politics are as far as economic policies go.

It's not unusual to find a working-class person making $30,000 a year or lower voting Republican. To a European political economist, this doesn't make any sense. Why are you voting for a party that seeks to reduce taxes on the wealthy and roll back regulations that, at least ostensibly, protect the poor and the ordinary citizen?

But they're missing one key element. America is an aspirational society. In other words, when you ask the typical working-class middle-American citizen who they are, they would tell you that they are more than their present physical and financial circumstances. They see themselves being able to achieve anything that they set their minds to.

In other words, you can come across people who make $30,000 per year who see themselves easily becoming millionaires. This is a far cry from places like India, the Philippines, or Europe for that matter.

I bring this up because people who are persuasive are able to zero in on what people aspire to because there are two ways to address somebody. You can talk to them based on who they are right here, right now.

They may be in a rough spot in their life, they may be going through struggles, they may be going through loss, and it's easy to frame the situation in such a way that things will never get better. So, the best thing that you can do is to have somebody help you. Somebody should give you something because they're in a better position. They are superior and you're inferior.

In many cases, that would work. But some people are aspirational. They don't see themselves as victims. They don't see themselves as needing a hand up and more of people requiring a level playing field.

In other words, they don't need your help. They just need the opportunity. These are two totally different things.

Expert manipulation must zero in on what people aspire for because it's very easy to get sidetracked and focus on where people are right now.

Let me tell you, if you phrase your message the wrong way, people will feel condescended to. They would say, "Who do you think you are? Are you looking down on me? Are you condescending to me? I can do what you can do. I may be in a tough spot in my life and I may have made bad choices, but ultimately, we're equal."

So you have to be very careful how you read people. And oftentimes, they often say things that are the actual opposite of what they really mean. In other words, there is a disconnect between how people behave and what their public values are.

For example, in certain parts of the United States, in particular the South, societal values like independence, autonomy and freedom are very big. They are bywords, if not slogans.

But when you look at the social welfare dependency numbers for certain parts of the South, it paints a completely different picture. In other words, people pay verbal homage to certain virtues, but when it comes to their actual decisions on a day to day basis, they're living a completely different reality.

So, you have to be aware of this. And it depends on you as to how you're going to approach this. Some people would appeal to people's stated values knowing full well that their actual reality is anything but their stated values.

Other people looking to convince would say, "Let's cut through the crap. Let's not play any games with ourselves. Let's get real." And then they would lay out how people actually behave and why this is a problem.

They would then lay out a different way and set of actions that would enable people who have certain challenges to make certain choices so that they can go to where they want to go and achieve the reality that they are capable of achieving.

You have to be able to read people's values. Otherwise, you're just going through a list and whatever positive results you might get is really the product of random chance instead of a systematic and methodical way of persuading people.

You have to be aware of what their values are and how they're living and what kind of internal narrative makes that work. You have to work with that internal narrative because if you were to disturb that, it's as if you're breaking the spell.

Do you think people react favorably when you break their delusion? Here's the spoiler, they won't like it.

This reminds me of the famous Greek philosopher Plato's allegory of the cave. There were these slaves that lived in a cave and their only perception of their identity was the shadow they cast on the wall of the cave.

There's a light source and they would see their shadow. They can't turn around. All they can see is the shadow.

It so happens that one day, one of the slaves was able to manage to become free. He was able to leave the cave and he saw the sun for the first time. When he came back to that cave and told everybody that the reflection they're seeing on the cave is a lie and that there is an actual sun out there and that is the true state of things, they didn't take it well. In fact, he was violently resisted.

The same applies to people who try to convince others by trying to be as real as possible. In theory that makes sense because hey, let's face it, in the Western world, truth is one of our highest social values. The ability to tell it like it is, perceive reality the way it is, unvarnished and unapologetic, is a high social value in the West, especially in the United States. In Asia, this is not necessarily the case.

So if you don't know your audience and you use the wrong tactic, or you try to cut through the social conventions of perceiving these external stimuli, you're viewed as a threat. You are resisted. In many cases, you are opposed.

Because let's face it, just like the prisoners in Plato's allegory, too many of us fall in love with our chains. It's so much easier to continue to believe in illusions and lies rather than to actually redo the world that you have made sense of, knowing full well that you don't know what lies at the end of the journey.

People, at the end of the day, are creatures of habit. We'd rather live with the devil we know than take a chance on the devil we don't know. And if you try to convince people by challenging their assumptions, and this cuts close to home because it erodes or it feels like you're eroding their values, get ready for a massive pushback. This is especially true when it comes to religion, spirituality, and ultimate life meaning.

But there are ways to get around this. There are ways to overcome the resistance so you are able to change people's mindsets. Once that kicks in, they start looking at the world's stimuli the way you would like them to see them. This then creates the necessary conditions for the emotional state that ultimately changes their actions.

Once you get people to change their actions, then that's when things get real because actions have consequences. Actions lead to a context that changes reality, and that's the ultimate goal of any kind of persuasion. Whether you call it manipulation or lying or haranguing, or simply talking and sharing, ultimately it's all about a changed reality.

Chapter 1: Offering an Alternative View or Reading of Reality

There are many ways to label this technique. Some are quite uncharitable. In fact, a lot of people would readily call this lying. Well, that is a judgment because there are many different forms of offering an alternative truth.

A lot of people would love to believe that the truth is the truth. But is it really? As I have mentioned earlier, two people can experience the same operative set of facts and walk away with completely different interpretations. Where's the truth there?

When you ask the person who said, "The rich are getting richer and the poor are getting poorer. There's no way I could afford that Ferrari," that's true for him.

When you look at his life or you train a camera on what happens in his life and the consequence of his choices, there's a high likelihood that he will never be able to afford a Ferrari because he already said, "I can't afford it. I don't have what it takes. It's not going to happen." That's the truth.

Is it necessarily a lie to say that? No. It doesn't have to be that way. Because that's exactly what's happening with the other guy.

The other guy asked a question, "How can I afford that Ferrari?" And when you ask yourself a question, you trigger your mind to start coming up with answers.

Well, first of all, you're going to have to get more money. Which then triggers another question: How much money do I need to make? Well, last time I checked, a Ferrari costs north of $250,000, okay?

So now we have a dollar figure. That begs the question of: How do I make that $250,000?

Well, you can work overtime at your current job, or you can go to school at night so you can get a higher paying job. You can start an online business or do freelancing on the side. You can change your budget so you pay yourself first instead of your bills.

You can also invest the money that you've saved up in riskier investments that increase your chances of doubling your money, or you can go into investment pools with other people.

My point here is not so much the specific questions, but the fact that these questions were triggered in the first place. Which leads to a greater possibility that you would be able to transcend your current material state.

The first person's flat out judgment that he doesn't have what it takes? Or this other person's series of questions that lead to more and more possibilities? Both of them are true. And that's why to say that manipulation is somehow lying is missing the point.

You can manipulate with untruths. You can do that. You can feed people distortions of facts or made up facts so they can interpret a neutral set of stimuli to do what you need them to do.

You will definitely be able to do that, and that's what people do. But that's a shortcut because they supply something that isn't objectively true and is harmful because it's a lie.

Seems pretty straightforward, right? Well, not quite. What if I told you that things that you may think are "a lie" can actually lead to good things? This seems like a delusion, but people actually do great things out of delusion.

What if you lived in a society that is convinced that women are worthless? There's no good in them. They're only good for children and not much else. That is the "truth" in that society.

Actually, in that society, people prefer a sexual relationship between men than a sexual relationship with women because women are just viewed as a means to reproduction. That is their "truth."

And then somebody comes along and says, "No. Women are valuable in and of themselves. They're not just a means to reproduction. They are inherently valuable in themselves because they are human beings."

That idea would be a lie to that society. That would create a disconnect and it would create conflict.

Now, you may be thinking to yourself, "Well, that society never existed." Well, I just described ancient Greece and Rome to you.

In fact, if we're completely honest, there are still certain societies in this so-called modern world where that is the thinking. Where's the truth there?

So, the whole idea that manipulation is really essentially a matter of lying or not lying misses the point. Instead, it's all about the ability to present an alternative truth.

In that context, in the sexist, misogynistic, patriarchal ancient Greek and Roman context, the alternative truth of the equality of sexes was revolutionary. It was a game changer.

Does this sound familiar? Well, it should. Because in our modern world, at least for most countries, the idea of one human being owned by another human being is repugnant. Slavery makes people sick.

But that hasn't always been the case. In fact, regardless of what society you're looking at, whether it's Japan, Europe, Africa, South America, Southeast Asia, Vietnam, the Philippines, Ukraine, or whatever country, slavery has been a constant.

Whenever there's a war and villages are captured, what do you think the winning army does with the losing territory's population? Well, first of all, depending on where it happens, the rule of thumb is to kill the men, and possibly even the boys.

And depending on where you are in the world and at what point of history, the next step is to rape the women and the girls. But there is one constant: slavery.

I raise this because slavery is the truth for so long. And then comes the "lie," or what I would like to say, the alternative truth of equality.

Believe it or not, the idea that it is morally repugnant for one person to enslave or own another person is relatively new. It has a recent vintage and it's very British, very Western, and very European.

In fact, in places like the Philippines, slavery was an accepted way of life up to the mid-1800s. In many parts of Africa today, that cultural practice still persists. Of course, it's underground and it comes under many different labels, but it's still slavery. What changed?

Well, it's all about that alternative truth. So, to say that the alternative truth of changing how people look at objective stimuli is a form of lying misses the point.

Effective persuaders are able to insert alternative truths into the thinking processes of the people whose behavior they're trying to modify. This takes skill.

Because as I have mentioned, oftentimes, when we detect our core assumptions being challenged, we overreact. Some people react more violently than others, but there is a reaction because nobody wants to change.

We're all creatures of habit. We've grown accustomed to thinking of and processing reality a certain way. And when we come across somebody with an alternative reading of what we define reality to be, we become uncomfortable.

And this doesn't have to involve lying as normally defined. But you can bet that people would say you are lying because this doesn't line up to how they define reality.

There are really two ways to deal with this. Good persuaders will look at how people look at a situation and they will find a way of inserting the alternative reading in such a way that it isn't interpreted as a threat.

How do you do this? Well, first of all, you can point out situations or possibilities where a person's belief system contradicts itself.

For example, if you're trying to persuade people that there is something morally wrong about abortion, you probably are not doing yourself any favors to say to them: "Abortion is wrong because all life is sacred and valuable." You can quote the Bible all you want and these people will not be convinced.

Now, if you take a different tack and you ask them if they believe in freedom, they probably would say yes. And if you ask them if they believe in choice, then you know they would say yes because the freedom to have an abortion in the United States is labeled "pro-choice."

So far so good. And you say to them, "Do you believe in non-discrimination?" and they would say yes because this is part of autonomy, freedom, liberty.

Now, when you say, "If you truly believe in everything you say and a woman has a choice over that fetus growing in her body, then you would agree that it's perfectly moral for her to abort that fetus because it's black or it's gay."

Now, in that logical setup, you work with their value system and you lead it to its contradictory conclusion, and then there's a disconnect. There is that opening in the logic sequence that gives you an opportunity to make the claim that "Maybe it's a bad idea to do that. Maybe there is inherent value in a human life, regardless of whether it's gay, black, white, poor, rich, abled or disabled. There is inherent value in life."

I hope you understand that this is not lying as we normally view it. Instead, it's an alternative truth that uses the mechanisms of logic in the minds of the people that you're trying to convince.

You have to work with these internal mechanisms, otherwise, you're not going to be all that persuasive. Instead, you come off as somebody who's just trying to browbeat them into your point of view. Unless you have a gun, it's not all that effective.

Logical Techniques

What are the methods you can use to position alternative truths to produce at least an awareness or a perception of a different conclusion? Well, you can use the logical contradiction approach that I mentioned above when it comes to abortion, but you can also use distortion.

In other words, if we look at the internal logic of a person's belief system, it leads to distortions and negative effects that they may not have been fully aware of. One good example of this is Immanuel Kant's philosophy.

Immanuel Kant came up with the concept of morality based on universal absolutes. He said that murder is murder regardless of whatever justification you may have. A crime is a crime.

And to bring home the point, he said whatever moral system you come up with, don't look at it from you imposing it on other people. Instead, look at it as a set of rules that you're not only going to impose on yourself or other people, but everybody else.

If everybody did that same thing, what would happen? Would there be a net positive good?

When you look at morality from this perspective, it makes a lot of sense. It's very practical. Because if we say it's okay to kill somebody else and we repeat that billions of times over and everybody does that, everybody dies. An eye for an eye leaves the whole world blind.

The same goes with stealing, adultery, and so on and so forth. You can use that sense of distortive effect when you make an argument that deals with other people's preconceived notions. You take their idea.

Remember, you're trying to present an alternative, but you're not going to make any progress if you just say, "My way is better." They're going to laugh at you. Instead, you look at what they already believe and you say, "Okay, let's apply that across the board. Let's blow that up. Make it a universal truth."

And what would be the effect? Well, the truth is, most people would like to believe in things where they benefit. In other words, it's a one-way street. They would like to get their cake and eat it too. They would like to have it both ways but forget everybody else.

So, when you come along and say, "Okay, this is what you want for yourself. This is how you set up this logical relationship. But if we were to apply that principle across the board and everybody gets to do it, would you be happy? The obvious answer is normally no.

So, this is one way of using alternative truth through the power of distortion to disrupt somebody else's belief system. Because remember, what you're trying to do is create an idea virus.

You know how viruses work? They are pieces of DNA, normally RNA, that plug into bacteria and hijack the nucleic machinery of bacteria to make copies of themselves. In fact, they make so many copies they destroy the old bacteria and all bits of DNA spread infecting other bacteria.

You're doing the same with ideas. You work your argument, it lodges into their internal logical machinery, and overrides it. So their conclusion is actually the alternative truth you're trying to present.

Now, what I described is just a neutral process. You can do this for malicious purposes, but you can also do this to open people's minds. And at the end of the day, being convincing or being more persuasive is really neutral.

It's a skill set. It's a tool. Just as you can use your computer to read the Bible, you can also use the computer to download porn. It's a tool. And the logical process that I just described is a tool. It's a means to an end, but you determine that end.

Be Careful of How You Manipulate Others' Opinion Because It Can Rewire Your Brain

According to a report published in the journal Nature Neuroscience in 2016, researchers found that congenital liars have altered brains. In particular, one part of the brain called the amygdala has a different response signal when people become habitually dishonest.

Usually, the amygdala is hyperactive when there is a disconnect between our claims to truth and what we appreciate of truth. In other words, if we are aware of certain facts that we think is true and we say or position the truth in a different way, our amygdala, through cat scans, would respond in a hyperactive way.

Habitual liars, on the hand, who willfully engage in dishonesty have a decreased amygdala signal.

Chapter 2: Denial

As I have mentioned earlier, you have to position your alternative facts or alternative truths to hijack the internal logical processes of your intended target or your audience. One way this plays out takes the form of playing up to their hopes.

You have to understand that human beings do not like to be wrong. If you don't believe me, when was the last time you got excited in a positive way when somebody said to your face that you were wrong or that there's something wrong with you?

I would venture to guess that it's been a long time ago or that never happened. Welcome to the club.

Human beings in general don't like to be wrong. And the human ego is so powerful that it would basically distort our perception of reality just so we can get away from the conclusion that we screwed up or made a bad decision.

In other words, this is a form of self-preservation. Psychologists call this "denial." This is a common feature of human psychology across the board.

It doesn't matter what country a person comes from, it doesn't matter whether they're rich or they're poor, gay, straight, abled, disabled, transgendered or cisgendered. It doesn't matter. All of us have the capacity for denial. It's like baked into our psychology.

If you're trying to convince people or you're trying to be more persuasive, one way you can get your message across and, more importantly, have people act on it, is when you hijack their tendency for denial. They know the truth.

For example, a child grows up with an alcoholic father who is very abusive. When that child becomes an adult and is able to buy his own home and raise a family of his own, many children would idealize their fathers. They would say, "I had a perfect childhood. Your grandfather is a great man." They're in denial.

It's not that they forgot when their fathers used to beat them in a drunken rage or slapped their mothers around in front of them. Instead, they don't want to suffer through the ego-bruising process of looking at reality.

They know that it happened, but they would rather imagine somebody to be different enough so they don't have to deal with the reality. We do this a lot. We do this with our jobs, our past performance, our past relationships, our education. I'm talking across the board.

Knowing this, persuasive people can hijack that very "normal" human tendency for denial to get people to do what they want to do. One common example of this are gym memberships.

I'm sure you have seen gym membership materials in your email telling you that your local gym is running some sort of sale and there's some massive discount available for you. You just need to show up.

So, when you show up, the sales person for the gym would tell you, "We have all these machines, and we have all sorts of Zumba, meditation classes, and spin classes that you can participate in."

And then they look at you and then they say, "Well, with the proper workout and if you adopt this system that we're going to give you which is absolutely free, you can lose weight, you can become more toned, and you can achieve your fitness goals."

They make a big deal of the concept of "fitness goals." That's a code word. When you think about it, the fitness goals ties into your sense of denial. You know that you're overweight and you're less active than you would like because of your lifestyle. You are at that point in your life.

And when somebody talks about fitness goals and talks about you being able to meet them if you use certain tools or adopt a certain diet or take out a gym membership, they're appealing to your sense of denial.

Because somebody who is not approaching you that way would say to you, "You're in bad shape. You need to adopt a program quickly and it's going to be painful. There's not going to be that many options involved. You're going to have to make serious sacrifices."

Now, listening to this is painful to a lot of people because they don't want to look at reality in the eye. They'd rather look at it from a perspective of having many different choices and adopting a healthier, more active lifestyle is just one option they could take because they feel that the world is open to them, or at least they would be approached that way. That is their denial.

But in reality, they need to take serious action right here, right now. Otherwise, that window of opportunity as far as their long-term health goes is closing rapidly. Once people hit the age of forty, that's when chronic diseases start to kick in. I'm talking about lifestyle diseases like diabetes.

But people don't want to hear that, especially in the United States. So a persuasive person would have to appeal to their sense of denial. And the most obvious form this denial takes is the idea of options and choices.

Once you get a person who comes into the door through the keyword-loaded email saying they would like to explore their health options, it's so much easier to get them to sign up to that gym membership. But in the back of your mind, you know that maybe they'll show up 3, 5, or 7 times, but they are on the hook for six months or even a whole year.

The main reason why gyms throughout the United States remain in business is because only a small fraction of people who sign up for memberships actually show up regularly. In fact, the typical gym in your state, your district, or your city, routinely overbooks their facilities.

For example, they only have ten treadmills, but they can book 100 members to use those facilities or even more and they don't need to worry. Why? Only a tiny fraction actually uses that equipment. And that's how gyms make money. It's all about plugging into this very human tendency to engage in denial.

People don't like to admit that they're doing wrong or that they've made the wrong choices. They'd rather have the fantasy continue and this makes them vulnerable when people plug in idea viruses that work with those internal fantasies.

People suffering from extreme narcissism are especially prone to denial tactics. This also works in a large-scale setting.

In the book "Long Term Capital Management" released in 2003, the author argues that the collapse of the long-term capital management industry in 1998 wasn't the product of poor decision-making processes or a simple shortage of crucial information. Instead, the industry imploded because of a shared sense of denial.

They couldn't see that the hedge fund bubble that these financial managers who were operating within wasn't all-knowing and all-powerful. And the problem with living in any kind of social bubble is you slowly start to believe certain things about your fixed social group that may not line up with reality as we objectively perceive it, and it's no surprise that certain industries would implode.

Another good example of this is the dotcom burnout in the early 2000s. In fact, a good argument could be made that the mortgage industry in 2008 whose problems triggered the credit crash suffered from a collective sense of denial.

And as alarming as this very human tendency may be, it is ultimately neutral because it can be worked with to present alternative truths and narratives that can lead to different outcomes.

Chapter 3: Tapping the Power of Shame

I'm sure you've of the story of The Emperor With No Clothes. In the interest of clarity, let me just give you a quick rundown.

Two con men tricked an emperor into wearing a new fabric the con men came with. The new fabric is invisible. In other words, when the emperor wears the fabric, he's completely naked.

One day, the emperor wanted to go out in the town in his new outfit made out of this wonder fabric. The con men came along with the emperor, and they were very confident and proud. According to the plan, nobody raised a fuss.

Here was the emperor, completely naked as the day he was born in broad daylight, and all these townspeople were bending their knee, honoring and giving praises to the emperor and everything was fine and dandy.

Then all of a sudden, out of nowhere, this little kid pointed at the emperor and said, "The emperor wears no clothes!" In a flash, it's as if everybody's stopped becoming blind, and they started laughing at the emperor.

There are many variations of this story, but it contains a very important truth that we can use in this book on persuasion and manipulation tactics. I'm talking about the Shame Factor.

Believe it or not, I'm not talking about the shame of the emperor who was butt-naked in broad daylight. That's too obvious. Instead, I'm talking about why this con job worked so well.

Can you imagine how outlandish that is? A completely invisible fabric and people would believe such a fabric existed? Even more incredible, a wealthy and powerful emperor falling for the lie, and wearing clothes made out of that fabric, and possibly paying a lot of money for it.

It all boils down to the very basic human fear of shame. You see, in the story, everybody went along with the lie because the con men said early on, "If you don't see the magic fiber of the material, you are an idiot."

That's all there is to their scam. They were relying on the fact that most people do not want to be considered idiots. Buffoons.

Ignorant. Morons. So there was a collective delusion regarding this artificial reality. Nobody wants to feel embarrassed, so they went along.

As fantastical as that story may be, it's happening today. If you don't want to be manipulated, it's a good idea to see how this plays out. It all boils down to shared delusions, just as individuals have personal delusions.

I've already covered this in the previous chapter. For example, your father might be an alcoholic and abusive person. Growing up, your dad may have called you all sorts of names, and destroyed your self-esteem.

As you become older, you don't want to be embarrassed or ashamed of your family history, so you make up all sorts of stories about how great your father was, how respectable and praise-worthy. In other words, you have a secret shame that you're hiding, so you engage in all sorts of denial.

Now, if you were to take those people who have those common issues, and you come up with a lie that caters to that psychological need, then you have group delusion.

Since you're feeding into their group delusion, you make the process even more bulletproof by saying that if you question the basic assumptions of this group delusion, there's something wrong with you. You're the enemy.

This happens quite a bit in wartime propaganda. If you've ever looked into how the Japanese media brainwash the whole population during World War II, a lot of this was going on. There is a "Us versus Them" mentality, and believe me, you don't want to be "them".

You don't want to be an outsider. You don't want to be an enemy. You don't want to be the traitor. If you think that since you're reading this book in America, that this doesn't happen in the United States, think again. It's only been a few years since George W. Bush said, "You're either with us or against us."

This type of thinking is all too common, and it's very easy to exploit. Its power arises from the fact that nobody wants to be an idiot. Nobody wants to be the outsider. Nobody wants to be the fool.

So even when we can see that the official truth or the official claims do not line up with the things that we can readily perceive with our eyes, ears, noses, tongues and tactile facilities, we go along. Believe me, the very human tendency to get along is all too strong.

How to use the Power of Shame to your advantage

To become a more persuasive person, you have to read your audience. You have to look at what they hold dear, what values do they subscribe to. How do they imagine themselves? Next, you look at that shared identity or value system, and you look at the taboo.

Now, this is a little tricky, because, in Asia, the taboo is "shame". In Asian societies, honor is very important. You don't want to bring dishonor to your family. Name is very important. That's why the Chinese and the Japanese have a term called "saving face."

In certain countries, this is stronger than others. It's not unusual to find out about Japanese government officials stepping down even in the case of very minor scandals. The power of shaming your family is just too strong. You don't want to let down your larger identity.

In the East, generally speaking, people have two identities. Their individual identity, and their group identity. Regardless of what you do, you don't want to bring shame and dishonor to your group identity.

In Southeast Asia, this is also at play but a slightly different level. For example, in places like the Philippines, if you go to a particular region, people don't consider themselves strictly Filipino. That's more of a theoretical construct than an everyday practical reality.

Instead, they consider themselves Ilocano, Cebuano, Mindanaoan, Ifugao, and if you drill deeper into the town level, then it gets even more clannish. So it's not just a simple matter of coming from Pampanga. Which part of Pampanga? Are you from Porac or Angeles? Where in Isabela are you from?

This might seem like a simple matter of geographic origin, but it brings with it all sorts of societal expectations. The Chinese are like this as well. There's a big perceived difference between Chinese from Fujian and Henan.

You can see the importance of this perceived group identity when you go to the United States, and you see Ilocano community groups, Hainanese and Fujian people. You might be thinking that this is just a social grouping for social get-togethers and town celebrations. No. It has a deeper importance. It all boils down to trust.

Fujian people are more likely to go into business with other people from Fujian province. They test this by how well you know the language. This is why the Hokkien dialect is essentially the lingua franca of business in Southeast Asia because a lot of Fujian-Chinese emigrated to Southeast Asia and became very wealthy.

A lot of their secrets to success is that they do a lot of deals with fellow Fujianese. I'm sharing this with you because when you know your audience, you can see the importance they place on staying within certain safe circles of identity, and outside of that circle is shame. One example of this is African-Americans.

Now, when you're dealing with Africans who came to America, you're most likely dealing with people who have middle-class values. Very different from African-Americans who were descendants of slaves.

In that latter group, there is a documented social pattern where if people think you're acting white, you will be the object of ridicule.

It's not unusual for poor and working-class American blacks to simulate ignorance or low-level academic performance out of fear of "acting white".

It doesn't matter what your interpretation of this may be. My point is, shame is a very powerful force. If you know how to set up your offer in such a way that it can tap into the power of the all too human fear of shame, you become more persuasive.

You might not be able to get them with logic. But you might be able to get your point across through fear because nobody wants to be the outsider. Nobody wants to be marginalized. Nobody wants to be pushed to the periphery. We all want to fit in.

We all want to be at the core, and this is why we all want to be called normal instead of abnormal. We all want to be popular instead of being unpopular.

So shame is a very powerful persuasive tool, but you have to be very observant, and you have to know quite a bit about the value system of the audience you're appealing to because you can't overstate your case and look like you are preaching to them or out to sow division.

This is quite a tight rope that you're going to have to walk.

Chapter 4: Diversion

When you talk to lawyers, it's very easy to walk away with the impression that the law is so well thought out and so seemingly objective, that any legal dispute would have a clear answer. After all, lawyers like to talk in terms of precedent and law.

Legislators come up with the law and it gets approved, and it's broken down into elements. When people go through a dispute, the facts of the matter can be broken down to fit into these elements, and people with average intelligence would be able to say that there is a likely outcome because the law seems so objective, rational and clear.

If only things were that way. You see, the mark of a great lawyer is not so much how well they know the law, but how well they can create diversions. It's not unusual for a lawyer with a lousy case, and I'm talking about the facts that don't fit into the elements provided by the law that guarantee some sort of relief. It's just not there.

Let's take the case of negligence. The legal elements of negligence are duty, breach, causation, and damages; or contracts, offer acceptance and consideration. If one of the elements is missing or debatable, the lawyer would make a big deal about vagueness, but more likely, they would divert the attention of the other party to their strong points.

What this does is it keeps the other persons' awareness off-centered. They don't see that the element is missing so that the attorney cannot make his or her case. They have no case, but the attorney was so good at making a diversion that the other side becomes more motivated to settle.

In the United States, upwards of 90% of cases settle, or they go to some sort of alternative dispute resolution like mediation or arbitration. The litigation that you see on TV shows like Perry Mason or LA Law is very rare.

Diversion is all about highlighting vaguely related or subsidiary or ancillary issues to take attention away from your mistakes, shortcomings or defects. This is a very powerful persuasion technique that you can use when you're trying to promote a product, or in the case of an attorney, trying to make a case that has serious shortcomings.

Now, of course, a lot of this is common sense. If your case is so bad that it's missing a lot of elements, you probably would not even take the case in the first place. The same goes for sales. If the product that you're trying to promote is defective or causes harm, you probably wouldn't be promoting it in the first place.

What I'm talking about here are cases and products and services that are somewhere in the middle. There's a lot of grey area, it can go either way. If you're good at diversion, you can increase your likelihood of a sale. You boost your chances of winning your case.

So how does diversion work? Well first, you have to breakdown the features of the product that you're trying to sell. For example, if you're dropshipping a product from China, your main selling point is probably the price.

Maybe you can make a big deal out of the shipping. Chances are, your weak points are going to involve originality of design, level of innovation, durability and possibly even overall quality.

To successfully manipulate your target audience members to pay more attention to your strong points, you have to divert their attention to the shortcomings of related products you are competing against. Make a big deal of the fact that Product B possibly made in the United States, cost 10 times more.

There is an art to this because you're not going to compare let's say, a mouse that costs $5 from China, with a mouse from the United States that costs $7. That's not going to help you. You're going to have to look for the most extreme case.

So usually, expert sellers would take a product that roughly has the same function, but is a specialized product, that's why the product costs so much, and you make a big deal of the fact that it's made in the United States.

In the mind of your target customer, you're trying to get them to link the origin of the product at a high price. You're pushing them through this diversion of thinking that I can overlook the fact that this drop-shipped item from China is kind of shoddy, badly-designed, and possible flimsy.

It might not even last that long, still, since it only costs $5 and the competing product let's say from New Jersey or Wisconsin, costs $75. So you see what's going on here? You have to understand that your target audience is not stupid. You're not doing yourself any favors by assuming they are.

Diversion is not about appealing to stupidity, instead, it's about triggering a rational decision-making process based on the wrong parameters. When you're buying a mouse, you should look at its durability and stability to get the job done.

You shouldn't pay as much attention to the price. What you are doing is you are diverting to the price factor and contrasting your offering with something that is so exaggerated but real. You're then hijacking the logical thinking process of your audience members so they conclude the way you like.

This is a very powerful tactic, and I've seen it happen again and again. If you want to see a good example of diversion persuasion, check out those late-night infomercials where the presenter would show an exercise machine with a model that looks like she's having a good time using the machine.

And then in the next segment, they would show somebody trying to do the physical activities that the machine automates fully or semi automates, they look like they're going through an ordeal. The alternative segment is so extreme that it looks like the person is going through a tremendous amount o pain.

The whole idea here is to create such a distinction that you are diverted from the factors that you should be paying attention to. This is the reason why those infomercials are so successful. In fact, in the 1980s through the 1990s, the average mark up for infomercial products is around 1000%, and they sold like hotcakes.

So, understand the power of diversion, how to set up conflicts that would divert from your weaknesses because remember, there is no such this as a perfect product. There will always be room for improvement, and there will be gaps.

You know you're a lousy salesman when your customer can easily see the gap in whatever it is you are selling.

Chapter 5: Seduction

Usually, when people think of seduction, they often imagine somebody who has a golden tongue, especially when it comes to members of the opposite sex.

If you ask the average person to define seduction, you would often get the impression that they believe that it can be encapsulated in knowing what to say or do at certain times. While that is correct, it misses most of the picture.

You have to understand that seduction is a series of signals sent according to a certain timeline. There is nothing formulaic about it. It's not like there is some sort of logical if/then process.

For example, if a woman looks at you a certain way, then you do this. And then this triggers this type of reaction, and then you do that. At the end of the process, the guy gets what he wants. It doesn't work that way. That's how the movies portray seduction.

If you think about it, they're forced to do that because if you were to come up with a realistic portrayal of seduction, it takes a lot of time. It also takes several tries at many different situations. In many cases, it would seem rather random.

But the truth is, when it comes to persuasion, getting people to do what you want them to do even though they might not even like what you want done, you have to know how to seduce people.

And in terms of persuasion, seduction is broken down into the ability to respond to the signals sent to you by your target as they, in turn, react to changing situations. Do you see the difference between this realistic definition of seduction and what you've been led to believe?

There is nothing formulaic about seduction because it really boils down to a very flexible skill set. You have to know how to read people, and more importantly, you have to read their context.

Guys who are able to take home women almost right after they meet them are not super geniuses. In fact, you can easily figure this out the moment they open their mouths.

Interestingly enough, a lot of them are not exactly lookers. They are not the second coming of Brad Pitt nor George Clooney.

By the same token, they don't own a Ferrari or a fancy sports car. A lot of them don't have much money.

So why are these guys so seductive when they seem to lack the typical background and resources a lot of people think are crucial to seduction? The truth is, seduction is a way of communicating. And what makes it tricky is that it doesn't just involve words.

You have to understand that when you're communicating with people, 80% of the persuasive signals that you are sending out do not involve a single word. That's right. You don't even have to open your mouth and you are already sending 80% of your message.

This is why a lot of people are puzzled when they seem to bring out the worst in others. They say to their friends, "Well, I didn't even say anything. I just showed up and I get all these negative vibes. And when I started talking, it just got worse. What's going on? Is it just me?"

Well, the longer you remain ignorant of the nonverbal signals you send out and the power of "conversing" with people based on nonverbal signals as well as situational reactions, the more you will suffer misunderstandings.

Let's get one thing straight. You may have a way with words, you may be able to collect your thoughts and communicate them in a clear unmistakable way, you might even be a great speaker, but until you master the 80% of the equation that involves nonverbal signals, you're going to be settling for crumbs.

You really will be. There are no two ways about it. You have to master context.

One of my friends in college was just amazing with women. It didn't matter where the female came from, what social background, how intelligent she was, or even how cynical she was.

He's often brought home women who are very jaded at guys. They really have their guards up, but he was still able to get together with them.

He told me one night, after a few drinks, the secret that he's been trying to hide all this time. He said the reason why he was so seductive is because he is able to target the right women at the right time with the right signals.

Let me tell you, the first time I heard this, I thought my eyeballs were going to pop out of my skull because I was rolling my eyes so hard. I was not exactly thrilled with what I heard because what he said was so generic. Tell me something I didn't know.

I thought that he was just trying to blow smoke and trying to play all sorts of games, but he cut through the misunderstanding when he said, "Listen, the first step in seduction is to find the right audience."

In other words, if you go into a room and it's filled with members of the opposite sex, not all of them are there to hook up. Not all of them are looking for love relationships. Not all of them even want to talk to people they don't know.

I didn't want to hear this lesson, but in hindsight, this was solid gold. I know a lot of people, including myself, who really try to impress themselves on people who don't really want to hear the message.

And I'm not just talking about a romantic or dating setting. I'm talking about sales, persuading bosses, trying to rally coworkers towards one objective instead of another.

And when I think back to this piece of advice, I can see why I didn't come up with the results that I had hoped. It's hard to be seductive when you are targeting the wrong person.

The second thing my friend told me involved reading the situation. You have to look at the vulnerability of the people that you are dealing with. They have to be susceptible to your message.

Let me tell you, if you have a disruptive business plan or set of objectives for your company, you probably will end up talking to a wall if the company is doing great. You can take that one to the bank.

As the old saying goes, it doesn't make sense to change horses when you're in the middle of a stream. Things are going well. You're in the middle of a process and your horse isn't dying, so what's the point of changing of horses? What's the point of taking a radical turn?

On the other hand, organizations are all ears when it seems like the company's collective back is against the wall.

Pay close attention to context because the context can help you be more persuasive because the person you're talking to or the organization that you're dealing with doesn't feel like they have much of an option.

The third step to seduction is proper management of all the signals that you are sending out. This is crucial. This is especially true when it comes to dealing with members of the opposite sex.

In the West, western women are honed in on a guy's level of confidence. Let's face it, there are a lot of guys out there who are faking it to try and make it. They try to be somebody they're not. They look like they have got something to prove, they try to look at slick and polished, but everybody knows the game.

And that's precisely the position a lot of these women are coming from because they're looking for one slip up. They're looking for one telltale sign that you're not who you claim to be. And a lot of this goes back to confidence.

Because ultimately, whether you are trying to seduce a member of the opposite sex or you are trying to convince a decision-maker, people are looking for a feeling. They make a quick association between a feeling that they get from somebody compared to a feeling that they get from another person. And these feelings are not emotionally neutral because they lead to certain decisions.

Women like to be made to feel that they are comfortable, secure, and they're going places when they're around a guy. Similarly, when an organization is trying to select between two potential leaders, the decision-makers like to feel that they're going somewhere so they'll go and elect the person that would give them that feeling.

In many cases, organizations are looking for a sense of emotional urgency paired with clarity. These are all parts of the seduction process because these can be manipulated.

People don't feel confident, secure, safe, protected and taken care of in a vacuum. You have to trigger it. Of course, a key part of this are the words that you bring to the table. But 80% is also due to the aura that you create when you say the right things in the right context to the right people to trigger the right chain reaction.

Remember, you're not just talking into a wall or the void. Instead, you are talking to people or decision-makers who have something else to say.

They have their own point of view and this interaction of the message you're sending and what they're feeling should lead them to feel secure with you, or at least feel better with you than somebody else. This is crucial. And this is what a lot of people miss when they try to be seductive.

Seduction is all about laying out the necessary conditions to elicit a feeling of security, control, partnership, and confidence. I'm sure you're not all that thrilled to partner with somebody who makes you feel insecure, small, beleaguered, embattled, or even defeated. Last time I checked, those weren't exactly sexy nor attractive emotions.

Understand this when trying to seduce an individual or a group. They are looking for a feeling. And here's a secret (on top of the other secrets that I already shared): that feeling is collaborative in nature.

Wrap your mind around that word. Collaborative. In other words, forget about that Hollywood idea of "the golden boy" or "the man with the answers" or Don Juan or Casanova walking into a room and just imposing his will. It doesn't work that way.

You just set the trigger and people fill in the details.

That's why when you go to a typical dance club or a get together or a bar, you would notice that there a lot of guys out there who don't look all that good with a goddess hanging on their arm. That is the art of seduction because they trigger the chain reaction that leads to that feeling. And it all begins with selecting the recipient of your message.

Now, in a business setting, this is pretty much done for you. Seriously. When you go into a business meeting, you can do your research regarding the company, where it's headed, what its problems are, and you can pretty much lock in on the kind of messages they want to hear.

If the company has been bleeding red quarter after quarter, they are ripe for one type of message compared to another company that is on its way to the next level on a rocket ship. You're going to have to present a different aura and message depending on who your audience members are.

And at the end of the day, it is their reaction and your reaction to their reaction that cements or unwinds the seduction.

Have you ever talked to a member of the opposite sex and things were going well, and all of a sudden you misheard or misunderstood what he or she said? Guess what, that upward spiral quickly stopped. It stalled, and then resulted in a downward spiral. It's as if nothing you could say and do can reverse the process.

This happens in a business meeting setting as well.

You have to pay close attention to the nonverbal signals you are sending out. This means your body language, how quickly you talk, the tone of your voice, eye contact, body positioning, the angle of your body, your clothing, your hairstyle, the accessories you choose to wear, and so on and so forth.

When it comes to reaction, it's really important to let the other side respond. You know you're dealing with a worthless sales person when they basically just recite their sales pitch to you. You can't get a word in edgewise. That's a lousy salesperson.

A good salesperson will spoon feed you the information you need to hear or look like you want to hear, and then they wait for your reaction. Then they respond with a little bit more information, and then they will wait for your reaction.

So, you're basically filling in the sales process for them. That's how you create a seductive environment.

Because at the end of the day, most of the products currently on the market are generic. Seriously. The only thing different between them is the brand.

And it's the mark of a really good salesperson to let the customer fill in the imagined value of the brand. This is only going to happen when you allow the back and forth to play out and the prospect develops that feeling that will enable you to convince them 100%. They want to feel secure, confident, in charge, relieved, hopeful, and ultimately, understood.

Of course, this is not going to happen overnight. You have to practice repeatedly. At the end of the day, you have to set up mechanisms in your pitch as well as in the setting that repeats your message over and over.

Repetition is a key part of seduction, but you cannot sound like a broken record. You have to set yourself up in such a way that wherever the prospect looks, they can see a repetition of your messaging.

Chapter 6: Minimization

Minimization is all about playing down the unattractive parts of your offer or bad events that you're responsible for. Whatever the case may be, minimization is all about shifting the attention of the target to the positive aspects of the situation you're presenting. A classic example of this involves sales people.

Let's face it, if you're serious about getting the very best product, you already have your homework done for you. Why? The top brands in a particular market vertical didn't become top brands by accident. It takes a lot of money, time and consistent performance to become a top brand.

Also, brands don't just arise out of nowhere because one company had a lot more money than another company. Instead, the customer base itself will organically select the top brand.

This doesn't always happen as planned and this doesn't always happen quickly. But eventually, the cream rises to the top. It's hard to manipulate open markets.

Now, in a closed market, it doesn't work this way. In a closed market, the monopoly brand always wins out regardless of how many people complain about its quality or its shoddy selection. It's the only game in town that's why these kinds of things only happen in a monopoly setting. But in an open market setting, the market has an uncanny way of selecting the very best.

If you're trying to sell a product, this is going to be a problem because if you are reaching out to people who have done their homework, they would already know what the top brands are. This is where minimization comes in.

Minimization is the persuasion tactic of downplaying the strengths of a competing product, competing idea, or competing suitor. Instead, you emphasize the strong points of the argument, product, or value proposition you bring to the table. These have to work together simultaneously.

This is where a lot of people stumble when they try to use this persuasion tactic. They think that minimization is just all about degrading or even downright dismissing or insulting somebody else's product or position.

That's just going to make you look like a hater. Seriously.

If you don't work on the other end of the equation, which is to highlight what you bring to the table, you're just going to look like a very negative person who just has a chip on his shoulder. How credible do you think you would look?

Here's the spoiler: not very. People could see that you just have an attitude problem. You're not really solving any issues.

Effective minimization is strategic. You don't want to come off as a flat-out hater, a negative person, or some sort of sour puss. That's not going to help you. Instead, when you are making your case, you have to make it look like the strong points of your opponents is part of a larger context.

One way to minimize is to compare a competing brand with another brand (normally not yours) that is so vastly superior. This happens in the automotive industry a lot.

If you're trying to sell, let's say a Honda, and somebody is looking at Volkswagens and other European cars, to minimize the option that your customer is currently considering, you should compare the strong points of that option with a category leader.

So in the automotive context, you would say, "Well, that Volkswagen looks good, but it's not as good as a BMW. It can't hold a candle to a Mercedes."

You say this because you know that the brands that you mentioned are, number one, objectively superior but, number two, carry a heavy price tag.

Your prospective customer would readily agree with you because they've already heard of BMW and how awesome they are. They already know that Mercedes Benz is one of the highest manifestations of German automotive engineering excellence. They get all that. But they also know their budget.

But you see what happened here? When you compared, you distracted them from the strong point of the Volkswagen they're looking at. This is where you come in and you play up the strong point of your value proposition.

If you're trying to get the person to buy a Hyundai, for example, make a big deal of the fact that Hyundai guarantees its power train for a full five years. That's unheard of. Let them know that this kind of offer is unheard of.

You then play up and maximize the significance of that point. What is the significance of a guarantee? What's the big deal about a company that would extend their warranty to something that is just ridiculously long?

Well, it doesn't take a rocket scientist. It means that for a company to back up its handiwork and craftsmanship for an extended period of time, they must be confident that this product will withstand the test of time. In other words, it's all about quality.

So, when you play up that factor, you underhandedly undermine the strong point of your competitors. You communicate to the prospect that the product that you are bringing to the table actually matches the product that they are seriously considering.

Minimization works, but you have to do it the right way. You can't just flat out minimize the option that your prospect is already looking at. It's going to make you look bad. It's going to make you seem like you have some sort of agenda.

If the prospect gets that impression, it would be very easy for them to dismiss you as, "Oh, you're just trying to sell me on a car." How credible and authoritative do you think you would be after that point?

Minimization is all about comparison and context. It also has to be paired up with an alternative. And that's where playing up the strong points of the solution or option you bring to the table works best.

Chapter 7: Guilt Trips

It's easy to see how guilt trips can cause people to pick one option over another if we're talking about personal matters.

If you're talking about something that involves a person's past relationships, it's quite easy to pick out decisions or situations that your target might feel guilty about. Maybe they feel like they've fallen short, they could have done more, they could have chosen better. or they could have paid more attention and possibly have come up with a better result.

The reason I can say this is because all of us have regrets. Seriously. Even the most seemingly well-adjusted person you come across will have some sort of regret.

If we could all agree that our world is imperfect and unfair, then it logically follows that regret will be part of the equation. Because if things were perfect, there's nothing to feel guilty or to be regretful about because everything would have fallen into place the right way and everything would have turned out well.

But we live in an imperfect world. People are imperfect. And that's why there is always regret.

Even if you're in a happy relationship, there is still some things that you would regret. At the very least, you would regret that you did not meet that perfect partner sooner. Even if you're happy with your job, maybe you would regret that you didn't apply for that job sooner.

Regret is a part of the human condition. And the good news for people looking to be more persuasive is that regret can be used to emphasize and amplify the power of your argument or suggestion.

A lot of people look at this process as necessarily bad. They look at it as a guilt trip. You are riding somebody's guilt to override their normal resistance to your ideas or suggestions.

Fair enough. But we live in an imperfect world and I would be remiss if I didn't tell you that guilt and regret can be avenues of greater persuasion.

Find Out What the Person Regrets

When you're targeting a sales prospect or a member of the opposite sex and you're thinking of using guilt as an avenue for greater persuasion, the first step is to figure out what they regret or what they have misgivings about.

The funny thing about this stage is that most people will actually volunteer this. Seriously. Even if you meet people who seem to be successful and who seem to have it all, they will volunteer certain aspects of their lives and certain personal details that they're not all that 100% happy about.

I once met a man who was extremely wealthy. I'm talking about living in the best part of town, driving really awesome cars, and living in a huge house. How huge was it? Well, let's put it this way, he not only had a volleyball court, a basketball court and bowling alley in his home, but he also had a tennis court.

I couldn't quite make full sense of his home. Part of me could swear that it was some sort of sports complex, but my eyes were telling me that it was just a large mansion. He seemed to have it all.

So, when I was talking to him as part of a company project that his contractor company was involved with, we met for lunch. And when he was talking about himself, he would talk about situations when he was bullied at school.

He came to America penniless and fatherless. Apparently, his father abandoned the family and his mother moved heaven and earth to get to America for a better life.

And then I asked him certain questions about his childhood and again, there was this unmistakable tinge of sadness, remorse, and guilt. He said he wasn't much of a student, so he slacked off. He got lousy grades.

High school was an ordeal because he just wanted to work, but his mom had other plans. His mom pushed him against his will to work hard at school so he can get into one of the top colleges in his state.

Sure enough, he was able to get in. He told me he didn't want to disappoint his mother, but when his mother told him that he should work for this large company because he got this diploma from this college, he said, "No. I'm going to put my foot down and I'm just going to work for myself."

That was his first company and he sold it for several million dollars. And then he formed two other companies, and made millions off of those. But I could tell.

When he was talking to me about going against his mother's wishes, there was a lot of guilt there. I was trying to read him, and there was definitely part of him that is driven by remorse, guilt, or "what could have been."

During that discussion, I thought I saw the glimmers of that guilt factor, but it really crystalized in my mind when he started talking about his past relationships. This really blew me away because it just kind of came out of left field.

I didn't ask any questions regarding that, nor did I appear to be somebody who's prodding to get in that direction. He volunteered it. To me, that is a clear sign that there was something about those past relationships that didn't quite sit well with him. Here was this guy, married to a beauty queen, for all practical purposes, talking about past relationships.

To cut a long story short, I was able to convince this prospect to go with our company because of our potential. How did I make that happen? How did I make this crystal clear?

Well, I laid out certain key verifiable events in the past involving his competitors. I told him that one of his competitors didn't do a deal with us and we ended up with another company that actually ended up buying them.

His eyes got really wide when he heard that because it's an open industry secret that I followed up with another similar story.

The subtext of my "stories" was actually quite obvious, at least as far as I was concerned. I wanted to appeal to his sense of regret. These were once in a lifetime deals. They're not going to happen again.

He knew he had opportunities in his past and I was appealing to that emotional core of not wanting to be left behind and to be left wondering what could have happened or what should have happened.

I'm happy to report that after that talk, he approved a series of other meetings that eventually led to a very mutually profitable partnership between the company I worked for and his company.

My point here is that you have to be aware that many people are prone to feelings of regret and guilt. You're not trying to play a guilt trip on them necessarily. Instead, you want to capitalize on the core emotion underlying guilt.

What is that core emotion? Well, nobody wants to be left behind. Nobody wants to feel abandoned. Nobody wants to feel like they're going to have to revisit what could have happened if they decided a different way.

Those are the complex emotions that I was tapping into when I told him the stories of the company's previous deals.

In the eyes of a third party who could have walked into our conversations, this was just a simple case of one person telling another person a story. But I can tell from the eyes of that multimillionaire I was talking to that I was speaking the language of missed opportunities, and ultimately, regrets and guilt. And he read me 100%.

It was crystal clear to him because he doesn't want it to happen again. He didn't need the money. Instead, he was looking after a sense of emotional closure.

Because that sense of guilt that he had will never go away. His father left him. The abandonment is real and that is part of who he was. The same applies to being a foreigner in a new land.

But when you see how people navigate these issues, you would be able to reposition the value proposition you bring to the table in such a way that they can read it crystal clear.

Chapter 8: Rationalization

Usually, when people rationalize their decisions, they play all sorts of logic games on themselves to make their decision look like something it isn't.

In a recent research study, behavioral researchers found that most people actually make emotional decisions. Put simply, they decide based on impulse.

Maybe a particular option makes them feel better. Maybe they are reminded of a happy memory. Maybe they are just choosing in the heat of the moment. Whatever the case, the participants knew that they were being impulsive or they were letting their emotions get the better of them.

But when they were presented with a forum to explain why they made the decision they made, the researchers found that people would often find logical-seeming explanations. This is rationalization.

People would bend over backwards and go through many hoops to claim that they made their decision in a purely logical and rational way. How come? A lot of this is due to the fact that people don't like to feel that they are out of control.

Most people associate emotional decision-making with lack of control. You know you're making the right call and you are being guided by the right criteria, factors, or motivations when you're using logic and reason in your decision-making process.

In the West, this cuts to the core of our shared values. We prize rationality, logic and orderly decision-making. We're not all that keen about emotionalism or romanticism. But there's a disconnect between how people actually behave and what they think of themselves.

This is where rationalization comes in. It's an after the fact exercise that tries to change one's impression of their action or other people's opinion of their actions. No matter how you cut it, it's all about trying to present a picture of yourself that is more logical, reasonable, and orderly than the reality.

The reality is that you can be irrational. Welcome to the club.

Most people can talk a good game of how well-reasoned their decision-making is, but at the end of the day, when given a choice, they let irrational factors (oftentimes cutting against their own interest) override their reasoning capabilities and they make an impulsive decision.

A lot of people don't want to own up to this and rationalization is really just a public demonstration of why you came to the decisions you made. How can this help you as someone trying to persuade a target audience or customer?

Rationalization comes naturally to most people. And if you were to preempt your target customer's rationalization process, you can easily come off as a hero. How can you not? You're doing their job for them.

Basically, you're presenting an option to them that they would like to choose impulsively. There's just something about the option that, at the back of their heads, they want to pick but they know better.

They know that it's not the best or most rational and logical choice. They know it, you know it. This is where rationalization comes in. Instead of having them go through the rationalization process after the fact, you take matters into your own hands.

You have to understand that if you're going to wait for them to rationalize, then this means that they have to choose your product or option first. That's too much of an assumption to make. Maybe their better senses would kick in and they would say, "Okay, this is crazy. I'm not going to do that." And the likelihood of that happening is very high.

This is why a lot of experienced sales people never let the customer say, "Let me think about it." They know that if they give the customer a chance to think about the deal, the deal is off. Why do you think a lot of timeshare high pressure sales meetings involve a one-shot offer?

Basically, the sales person would say, "We're going to give you all these goodies if you sign up for our timeshare program, but we can only give you this offer today. You don't have an opportunity to call us tomorrow to reactivate the deal. This ridiculous discount that we're giving you is only available now."

They're putting a lot of pressure on you because they know full well that once you get out of that office, your rational side will kick in. You start to compare advantages and disadvantages, likelihoods, probabilities and percentages. In other words, reality starts to set in and something that looked like a really good deal in the heat of the moment starts to fade.

In fact, for a lot of people, it actually starts to look like a bad idea because with everything else being equal, you have other more pressing things to spend your hard-earned money on. That's why high pressure sales people would rationalize your decision for you.

This is how they "sell." It's not through a brochure, nor is it through a slick video. It's all about the rationalization process because they know, deep down inside, you're not all that comfortable with the choice.

If you ask a hundred people what their highest priority is, I can bet you that most of them would not say "timeshare." Call me crazy, but I have that sneaking suspicion that timeshare rentals are not going to be in the top ten of people's priority list.

Since people have this built-in capability of rationalization, you can use this to become more persuasive. You do this by anticipating the objections the other party will have. But you phrase it like an after the fact assessment of their decision.

You assume that they have bought the timeshare so you would say, "Well, when you look at all the other options available to you and the fact that this can increase in value when you sell it to another person who wants to timeshare, it's actually a good investment. Also, when you look at just how uncertain other investments are and since this is really based on real estate, this is actually more secure."

So, you go through the list of potential objections people have and you end up creating a picture that solidifies the wisdom of their decision based on certain assumptions.

Everything falls into place because everything seems rational. But you have to do it for them because if you're going to wait for them to pull the trigger and sign on the dotted line and get that timeshare, it may be too late because they might snap out of the emotional state they're in.

You have to strike while the iron is hot, and this is why rationalization as a persuasion tool or manipulation device is strongest when the prospect or the target is at an emotionally vulnerable state.

This plays out all the time at timeshare rental sales offices. Basically, you get a couple to sit down at the sales desk and you get them all excited about the amazing vacations they may have. This is cents on the dollar. They're saving a tremendous amount of money compared to typical hotels. What's not to love?

So, while their minds are drunk with images of them touring the pyramids of Egypt, the pyramids of the Mayans in Central America, or the snow-capped mountains surrounding Mt. Fuji in Japan, you lay out a rational presentation highlighting the benefits of the offer.

You talk about costs, you talk about investment value, and you talk about flexibility, and ultimately, you cap it off with a simple statement: "You owe it to yourself" or something similar.

When you do that, that simple statement actually encapsulates a lot of emotional states. When you say to somebody, "You owe this to yourself," you're basically recognizing and acknowledging that they worked hard for their money.

Maybe they feel like they're slaving for their money. Isn't it high time that they treated themselves to a little something special? After all that work and sacrifice, wouldn't it be a good thing to reward themselves?

In fact, by phrasing that final statement in the form of owing oneself, there's a sense of obligation. You're appealing to somebody's need for self-care, self-love, and self-respect. We're talking deep here. So, it starts out with a rational-sounding argumentation, but at the end, you finish with a bedrock of emotion.

Rationalization works, but you have to lay it out properly. You can't overstate your hand. You can't go over the top. You can't exaggerate. The key here is rationality.

In other words, it has to be reasonable. It has to be proportionate. You can't just say, "Well, you're going to save a million dollars!" How is that possible when the person doesn't have a million dollars and is not intending to spend a million dollars?

It has to fit the context of the target. Regardless, rationalization plays into basic human psychology that's why it's so powerful.

Chapter 9: Gaslighting

When you gaslight a person, you're basically sowing seeds of insecurity – either in that person himself or herself, or you're making that person doubt another person or another group. This is not a simple matter of being a hater or a gossip.

I'm sure you've come across somebody who just can't say anything nice about other people. It seems like any organization, school, or even family, has at least one person who seems incapable of saying anything nice about other people. Most people can see the flower and the rose. All these negative people could see are the thorns.

Gaslighting goes beyond negativity. Instead, it is a deliberate and strategic use of the power of doubt.

Make no mistake, given how faulty human memory could be, there is always space for doubt. Also, when we make judgments of other people based on our experiences and based on our logical thinking faculties, there's always a possibility that we made the wrong call or we came to the wrong conclusion. Doubt is a crucial component of the human condition and it's not going to go away.

If you come across somebody who makes a decision, there will always be space for doubt because at the end of the day, there is no rewind button for life. You make one decision after another, and once you make that decision, it's set.

You can make another decision in the future to revisit a previous decision, but the damage has already been done. At the very least, you have that memory.

Given this reality, gaslighting is a very powerful manipulation tactic that can help you become very persuasive. Why? People ultimately already doubt. They might not be blatant about it, but they're already doubting.

Because hey, let's face it, none of us is perfect. Can you say with all certainty that all your decisions are 100% correct? Of course not. Nobody can.

This imperfection has a twin. It's called doubt. You know that there's always room for improvement as far as your decision-making powers are concerned.

Gaslighting is all about using the power of doubt to enable the target to see your perspective.

Now, there are many ways to do this and there are many ways to interpret this. If you want to be uncharitable and unkind, you can easily make the argument that gaslighting is evil. Why? Well, you can use all sorts of techniques like misdirection, finding contradictions, and flat out inaccuracies, aka lying, to gaslight.

What you're doing is you're destabilizing and upsetting another person's belief system. You plant seeds of doubt and you reinforce them through repetition, and you kind of mix things up but you can poke contradictions. You can direct the person's attention to certain actions that you read in a very negative way.

There are so many ways you can make those seeds of doubt sprout into toxic plants in the mind of your target, but they all lead to the same place. They all lead to the delegitimization and undermining of their belief system.

This is the most negative way to look at gaslighting. But there's another perspective. It doesn't have to be all negative. What if the person believes in the wrong things? What if the person drew faulty conclusions from a certain set of facts?

When you perform gaslighting through planting doubts, you actually facilitate a process in which that person can hopefully revisit their conclusions.

Have you ever been wrong about somebody? Have you ever jumped to conclusions and made certain assumptions? Well, maybe you would start thinking differently if somebody else went through the time and hassle of planting doubts to essentially "help you reprogram" your mindset. In this context, they're doing you a favor.

The worst feeling in the world is to go down a path of personal destruction and only to turn around and say to the people who claim to love you, "Why didn't you tell me? You knew I was going down this path, why didn't you try to stop me? You knew that I was making one bad decision after another based on my faulty assumptions. Why didn't you give me a different perspective? Why didn't you have a word with me?"

It hurts to even say this because it hurts to be that person. You have all these people in your life who claim to love you, but for whatever reason, they couldn't bring themselves to have a word with you and to just basically show you that your belief system is wrong.

Now, if you're completely honest, you would know exactly why. Because oftentimes, human beings are egotistic. We don't like to be wrong, as I have mentioned previously in this book.

To a teenager, the worst thing you can do is to tell them they're wrong because they will double up on the foolish things that they're doing. This is just part of human nature.

It's no wonder, more often than not, people who are near and dear to us just let us go down our path of assumptions because they feel that if they get in the way and they try to have us question those assumptions that we might push them out of our lives. It's as if they fear losing us so much that they'd rather take the chance of us getting lost through our own faulty thinking and beliefs.

If you are trying to persuade others to rethink their assumptions, then gaslighting is not an evil manipulative tactic. Instead, it can be a helpful manipulation tool that would at least give the other person a shot at getting out from under the toxic effects of their mindset and assumptions.

I've already talked at length about the power of mindset and assumptions in the early parts of this book. If you want to remind yourself of just how toxic mindsets can be as far as practical day to day reality, read those sections again.

How to Use Gaslighting to Get People to Think Differently

The essence of gaslighting is a set of willful messages intended to get the target to reconsider their belief system. This can take the form of doubting their beliefs or looking at things with a fresh set of eyes.

As a society, we don't like doubt because, at some level or another, it reeks of weakness. But doubt is necessary because if you're going down the wrong path and you are perceiving certain things that you know point to the conclusion that something's wrong, your doubt enables you to make the decision and turn around.

Gaslighting is all about planting seeds of doubt, or, in the case of most people, spreading fertilizer on that doubt. Because as I have mentioned in the earlier section regarding guilt and regret, there is always a possibility that you decided wrong.

It doesn't matter how smart you are or how high your IQ is, there is always that possibility. Since that possibility exists, then doubt exists – or at least the possibility of doubt.

When you gaslight, you plant seeds of doubt. Here are just some basic ways people gaslight.

They Demand Proof of Things that Other People Assume

One of the most basic way to gaslight somebody is to pick apart their assumption. For example, somebody said, "Well, that's my dad. He's funny, but often insulting. But what can I do? He's my dad."

And then you can gaslight by saying, "Are you sure? You don't look like him."

Sounds harsh – and this is an extreme example. But oftentimes, by looking at basic assumptions, like you are genetically that person's son and looking at it with a fresh set of eyes can change one person's assumption.

Maybe if your friend who thought his father was his biological father found out that he was adopted or was a product of his mother's affair with somebody else, he would start looking at the father he recognized for most of his life in a different light. This might not necessarily be negative.

Asking for proof, even if it is met with corroboration, like let's say a birth certificate proving that the man who you thought was your father actually is your biological father, can open a lot of doors.

Think about it, you may have a problem with your dad because you think that nothing you do is good enough to him. You can't measure up to him. And a friend says to you, "Are you sure he's even your dad? Because you don't look alike."

And then you got documentary proof, or maybe you even got a DNA test and it came up positive. That can still open the door to a reassessment of the relationship and possibly you looking at your father with a different set of eyes.

Maybe the reason why he had such high standards for you is because he believes in you so much. Maybe he sees your potential and is really hopeful for your prospects and that's why he holds you to such a high standard.

Maybe the standard is not to beat you down, make you feel inadequate and small, but to push you up, knowing full well that, deep down inside, you have what it takes because he believes in you 100%.

Sometimes, these realizations can only be triggered by a reaffirmation of something that you assumed, like paternity, family lineage, or fitness for employment if we're talking about your job.

Gaslighting can Involve Intimate Knowledge

Another way you can plant doubts in another person's mind to get them to reconsider their assumptions is to mention intimate truths. For example, if a friend of yours shared a secret from the past, if you remind them of that secret and relate it to how they're behaving today, they might be very thankful.

Of course, this is very scary because you're cutting close to home, but they can be very thankful because you are bringing out a detail that means so much to them that can possibly trigger an emotional reexamination of what they think their priorities should be. Best friends do this all the time.

Gaslighting is More Effective When It is Repeated

I'm not talking about you sounding like a broken record just spitting out the same statement that erodes self-trust and self-confidence.

You can basically bring the target person's attention to the assumption that you're trying to question when you direct their attention to certain things that are happening in their lives right now. It doesn't have to be the exact same thing.

Most people are intelligent enough to be able to fill in the gaps and connect the dots. This seeming repetition coming from all over the place involving all sorts of details can remind them, repeatedly, about their faulty assumptions.

If somebody hired the wrong person at work and you are that person's comanager and coequal, it's going to be hard to just say to that person, "You hired the wrong person. You made a mistake."

How do you think you will be received? Probably not all that well.

But if you bring up the consequences of the bad hire's actions and the results of that person's decisions, it would seem like you're bringing up different things day after day, but it's actually going back to the same person. And before you know it, despite your comanager's ego, the scales on their eyes may finally fall off and they could see their bad hire for what he or she truly is.

Again, as I have mentioned repeatedly in this book, people do not like to be wrong. We take it as an insult to our ego. So you have to gaslight by reminding them or bringing to their attention different facts that lead to the same person or lead to the same decision, and they will fill in the gaps. This is called reinforcement.

Point Out Hypocrisy

Another way to erode somebody's trust in their belief system or to sow seeds of doubt to undermine a faulty belief system is to point out hypocrisy. Nobody is exempt from this, okay? Let's get that out of the way.

We all talk a good game, but at the end of the day, it's hard to find somebody who consistently behaves based on their professed ideals. This is good news for you if you're trying to gaslight somebody into reconsidering their belief system or the things that they assume to be true.

Basically, you would look at their actions and compare it to what they say they believe in. This brings home the point that if you can't bring yourself to act with integrity as far as your public beliefs go, then maybe you're actually doubting your beliefs. Maybe they're not as important as you think they are and this is a golden opportunity for you to reconsider your beliefs. This is definitely one tack you can take.

Chapter 10: Play the Victim

In our Western culture, we have a collective soft spot for the victim. Unlike other cultures that focus on concepts of honor and shame, the Western mindset has a special affinity for the underdog.

When somebody is being beaten up, marginalized, persecuted, or oppressed, there's just something in us that is triggered. It's as if our eyes become wide open and we get emotionally triggered. We emotionally interpret the act of being persecuted with being sympathetic.

Of course, this denies the possibility that some people are essentially just getting what they deserve. After all, the rules of the universe haven't changed all that much. What you sow is what you reap. And if the things that you sow culminate in you reaping a very bad harvest of shame, pain, loss, and oppression, who's really to blame? This is the reality.

But when it comes to perception, people from the West and areas of the world heavily influenced by the West has a soft spot for the victim.

Good luck with trying to play this game with somebody from a shame and honor culture. In such a culture, weakness is something to be avoided.

When somebody is being oppressed, it is because that person is weak. While at the end of the day they will still try to help the weak and the oppressed, the logic is different.

In an honor and shame society, people who are in a strong position or in a position of privilege are obliged to help those lower. But they will remind the person that they are helping, "In no uncertain terms I'm helping you because you are lower. It is my obligation because I am in a superior position. I'm helping you precisely because you are weak and I am strong."

Not so in the West. We help people because we see ourselves in the underdog. We see ourselves in the person being put upon, persecuted, and oppressed.

There's a certain allure to being a victim. But the problem is, as a society, we tend to assume too much, and it's no surprise why a lot people would rather play the victim. When somebody is a victim, there are less expectations on them.

When you convince other people that you're a victim, the last thing that they would want to do is for you to take responsibility because hey, you're already suffering. Haven't you had enough? Haven't you gone through enough? Why this added burden of responsibility and accountability?

It is no wonder that a lot of people, with everything else being equal, would rather play the victim because they don't want to accountability. They don't want to be measured by the same metrics as everybody else. They want a pass.

And you might think that this is despicable and very negative, well think again. In the Western mind, there is always a part of us that would like to be viewed as the victim because there's less expectations of us. We're less likely to be held to account.

We're definitely less likely to be viewed as the cause of our misery. After all, you're already the victim. Why should people blame you?

But I hope you can see how absurd this is. It's like somebody who drank copious amounts of alcohol all day, every day, 365 days a week, and then when they discovered that they have liver cancer or they have cirrhosis of the liver, they're the victim. What's wrong with this picture?

Still, as a society, we have a very soft spot for people who claim to be a victim that's why a lot of us would rather be the victim as well. Its advantages, in our minds, outweigh its disadvantages.

Manipulating and Persuading by Playing the Victim

When you play the victim, you basically are making the point that, "I did not cause my misery." It's just a claim.

Because a lot of people who are viewed by society as victims are not really victims because of cause and effect. The choices you make on a day to day basis are the causes and your life is the effect.

I know it's harsh to listen to. Who wants to be poor? Who wants to be in a loveless relationship? Who wants to live life without love?

I could go on and on, but let's get real. A lot of the times, the state that we find ourselves in are the products of our choices. That's why we play the victim. And that's why we have a soft spot for the victim.

And this has a very powerful persuasive effect. Because when you say that the shortcomings of your product is because of the bad actions of a third party, you look sympathetic. The customer is more likely to give you the benefit of the doubt.

It doesn't enter their mind that maybe you didn't file the right paperwork. Maybe you didn't even bother to think about doing things a different way so you wouldn't be in an inferior situation. Maybe you're just lazy.

Instead, all the customer can see is that, "Oh, you're a victim of circumstances. You got the short end of the stick so let me give you a break."

This is a very powerful persuasive tactic. Remember to use it in a positive way because it can easily be abused.

Also, please understand that when people feel that they got played because you overextended yourself by playing the victim, they're not very forgiving. Just as people have a soft spot for the underdogs of society, we also have a very strong tendency to preserve our sense of dignity and ego. And if we feel that we have been made a fool of, we're not very forgiving at all.

So, you have to make sure that you play the victim in a very calculated way. Don't make this your default position because it can easily blow up in your face.

Conclusion

Whether you want to become more persuasive or you want to avoid getting manipulated, knowing the ins and outs of key manipulation techniques can help you become a more effective communicator and organizer.

The bottom line is simple: be clear on your objectives and know the tools at your disposal so you can achieve the outcome you desire.

Whether manipulation is evil or good totally depends on your intentions and motivations. Just as a knife can be used to murder someone, it can also be used by a trained surgeon to save someone's life. It all depends on intention and motivation.

Regardless, learn the techniques described in detail in this book so you can become more effective in your dealings with others.

Copyright © 2019 by Nick Anderson

All rights reserved. No part of this book may be reproduced in any form without permission in writing from the author.

No part of this publication may be reproduced or transmitted in any form or by any means, mechanical or electronic, including photocopying or recording, or by any information storage and retrieval system, or transmitted by email or by any other means whatsoever without permission in writing from the author.

DISCLAIMER

While all attempts have been made to verify the information provided in this publication, the author does not assume any responsibility for errors, omissions, or contrary interpretations of the subject matter herein.

The views expressed are those of the author alone and should not be taken as expert instruction or commands. The reader is responsible for his or her own actions.

The author makes no representations or warranties with respect to the accuracy or completeness of the contents of this work and specifically disclaims all warranties, including without limitation warranties of fitness for a particular purpose. No warranty may be created or extended by sales or promotional materials. The advice and recipes contained herein may not be suitable for everyone. This work is sold with the understanding that the author is not engaged in rendering medical, legal or other professional advice or services. If professional assistance is required, the services of a competent professional person should be sought. The author shall not be liable for damages arising here from. The fact that an individual, organization of website is referred to in this work as a citation and/or potential source of further information does not mean that the author endorses the information the individual, organization to website may provide or recommendations they/it may make. Further, readers should be aware that Internet websites listed in this work might have changed or disappeared between when this work was written and when it is read.

Adherence to all applicable laws and regulations, including international, federal, state, and local governing professional licensing, business practices, advertising, and all other aspects of doing business in any jurisdiction in the world is the sole responsibility of the purchaser or reader.

www.ingramcontent.com/pod-product-compliance
Lightning Source LLC
Chambersburg PA
CBHW070653220526
45466CB00001B/413